ARIES:

A COMPLETE GUIDE TO THE ARIES ASTROLOGY STAR SIGN

Sofia Visconti

© **Copyright 2024 - All rights reserved.**

The content contained within this book may not be reproduced, duplicated or transmitted without direct written permission from the author or the publisher.

Under no circumstances will any blame or legal responsibility be held against the publisher, or author, for any damages, reparation, or monetary loss due to the information contained within this book, either directly or indirectly.

Legal Notice:

This book is copyright protected. It is only for personal use. You cannot amend, distribute, sell, use, quote or paraphrase any part, or the content within this book, without the consent of the author or publisher.

Disclaimer Notice:

Please note the information contained within this document is for educational and entertainment purposes only. All effort has been executed to present accurate, up to date, reliable, complete information. No warranties of any kind are declared or implied. Readers acknowledge that the author is not engaged in the rendering of legal, financial, medical or professional advice. The content within this book has been derived from various sources. Please consult a licensed professional before attempting any techniques outlined in this book.

By reading this document, the reader agrees that under no circumstances is the author responsible for any losses, direct or indirect, that are incurred as a result of the use of the information contained within this document, including, but not limited to, errors, omissions, or inaccuracies.

Subscribe To Sofia Visconti

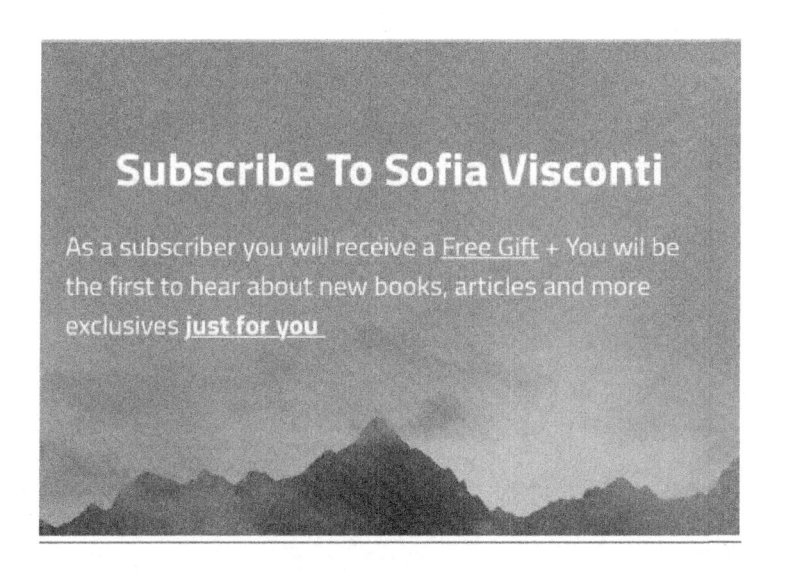

As a subscriber you will receive a *Free Gift* + You wil be the first to hear about new books, articles and more exclusives **just for you**

Click Here

Or Visit Below:
https://www.subscribepage.com/svmyth

Or Simply Scan The Qr Code To Join

Contents

INTRODUCTION 1
Aries Overview 2

CHAPTER 1: HISTORY AND MYTHOLOGY 5
Babylonians and Sumerians 7
Ancient Egyptians 7
Ancient Greeks 9
Evolution of "Aries" 10
Historical events 11

CHAPTER 2: LOVE & COMPATIBILITY 14
Aries Approach to Love 15
Compatibility With Other Zodiac Signs 17
Tips for Dating and Nurturing Relationships with Aries 23
General Tips for Dating and Relationships with Aries 24

CHAPTER 3: FRIENDS AND FAMILY 27
Aries as a Friend 28
Aries in Family Dynamics 30
Challenges in Friendships and Family 32
Developing Relationships 36

CHAPTER 4: CAREER AND AMBITIONS 38
Aries Career Preferences and Professional Goals 38
Aries Strengths in the Workplace 41
Challenges faced by Aries and strategies to overcome them 43

CHAPTER 5: SELF-IMPROVEMENT 49

Embracing Aries Strengths and Overcoming Weaknesses 50
Personal Development.. 53

CHAPTER 6: ARIES IN THE YEAR AHEAD 56
Horoscope Guide For Aries 56
Key Themes for the Year 58
Astrological Influences on Aries 59

CHAPTER 7: FAMOUS ARIES PERSONALITIES 63
Charlie Chaplin 63
Diana Ross 65
Robert Downey Jr. 65
Lucy Lawless 65
Thomas Jefferson 66
Mariah Carey 66
Eric Clapton 67
Lady Gaga 68
Elton John 68
J. P. Morgan 69
Maria Sharapova 69
Aretha Franklin 70

CONCLUSION 73

INTRODUCTION

Astrology has fascinated humanity for centuries. It explores the positions and movements of the planets and stars to identify their impact on human behavior and events here on Earth. Essentially astrology is a belief system that suggests a connection between the cosmos and our personal lives. In this book we embark on a journey to delve into one of the twelve zodiac signs, Aries. Inside we seek to uncover its secrets and gain valuable insights from it. The objective of this book is to offer readers an in depth exploration of the Aries zodiac sign. It aims to provide an understanding of the characteristics, traits and tendencies associated with individuals born under this fiery and dynamic sign.

Whether you are an Aries yourself or have friends or loved ones who fall under this zodiac sign, this book endeavors to assist you in navigating through their qualities and confronting any challenges that may arise.

ARIES OVERVIEW

- **Date**; Aries spans from March 21st to April 19th marking the beginning of the zodiac calendar.
- **Symbol**; Represented by the Ram. The powerful horns of a Ram symbolizes strength, determination and leadership qualities.
- **Element**; Aries is associated with the Fire element representing passion, energy and assertiveness.
- **Planet**; Mars, the planet known for action, aggression and desire governs Aries. This planetary influence amplifies their courage and competitive spirit.
- **Color**; Red.

PERSONALITY TRAITS

Aries individuals are recognized for their fearless nature. They possess the following personality traits.

- **Fearless**; Aries individuals fearlessly venture into new territories and embrace risks.
- **Energetic**; They radiate energy and enthusiasm often initiating ventures and exciting experiences.
- **Independent**; Aries value their independence and prefer to carve out their own path.
- **Leadership**; Aries are leaders at heart. They have a knack for inspiring and leading others.
- **Optimistic**; Aries maintains an optimistic outlook on life. Even in the face of challenges.

STRENGTHS

- **Brave**; Aries confronts challenges with courage and resilience.
- **Determined**; They possess unwavering determination to achieve their goals.
- **Initiators**; Aries takes initiative and excels at catalyzing beginnings.

WEAKNESSES

- **Impulsive**: Aries can be impulsive, often acting without thinking through the consequences.
- **Impatient**: Patience is not a virtue commonly found in Aries. They want things to happen immediately. They can become frustrated when things don't move as quickly as they'd like.
- **Competitive**: While being competitive can be a strength, for Aries, it can sometimes be a weakness. Their strong desire to be the best can lead to unnecessary stress and conflict, particularly in collaborative or team environments.

In the opening of this book we have delved into the realm of astrology with an emphasis on the Aries zodiac sign. So far we have gained knowledge about the aspects that define Aries including their birth dates, symbol, element and their ruling planet.

We have also explored the personality traits, strengths and weaknesses that distinguish individuals born under the sign of Aries. From their independent nature to moments of impulsiveness and impatience, Aries personalities are both inspiring and complex.

As we progress further into this book's core content you can anticipate a detailed exploration of Aries. We'll delve into its roots, connections as well as provide practical insights that will help you understand and appreciate the Aries individuals in your life. Together we will unravel the mysteries surrounding this zodiac sign by uncovering its stories, characteristics and compatibility factors. Join us on this journey as we unlock the secrets of Aries!

CHAPTER 1:
HISTORY AND MYTHOLOGY

The constellation known as Aries, has a captivating history that spans thousands of years. It has deeply influenced civilization with its origins intertwined in the records and observations made by various ancient cultures. To truly grasp the importance of Aries we must take a journey through time. Here we will explore how different civilizations perceived and depicted this marvel on their star maps.

In ancient times when the night sky served as both a storytelling canvas and a navigational aid Aries stood out prominently among the constellations. Its position in the heavens made it an integral part of tales crafted by cultures to explain the mysteries of the universe.

As we delve further into history and mythology we will uncover the tapestry of Aries revealing its role as a guiding light in the sky, a source of inspiration and a symbol representing cosmic awe for countless generations. Join us on this expedition to unravel the enigmas and meanings behind the constellation of Aries.

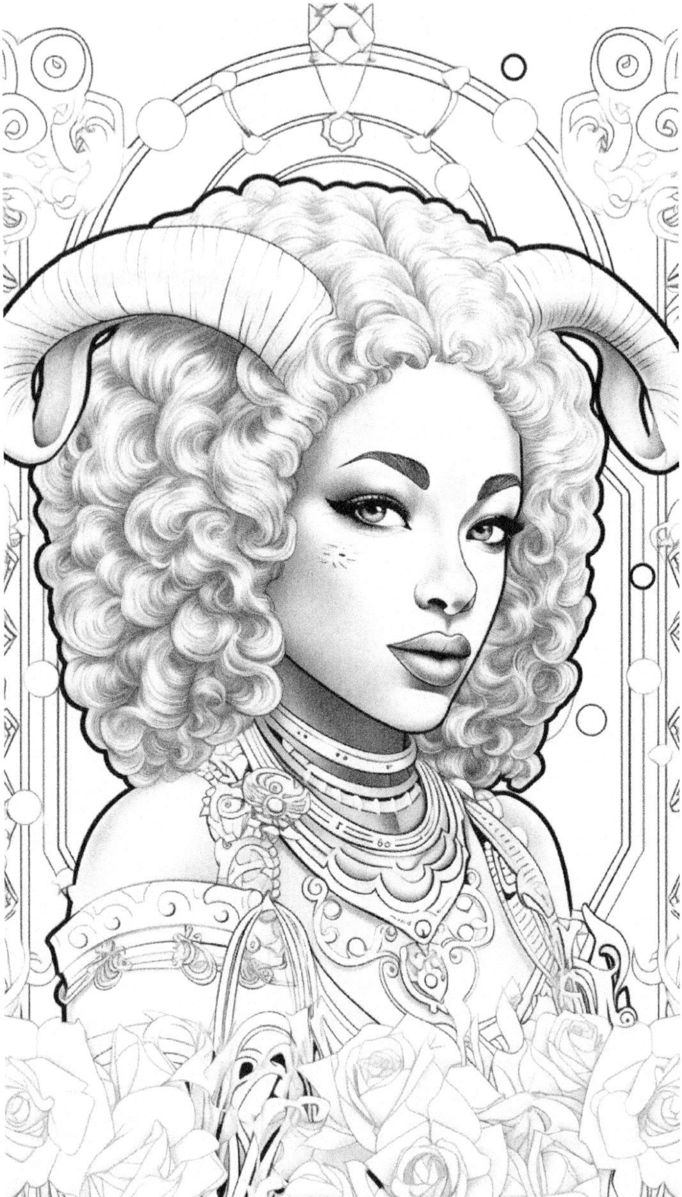

BABYLONIANS AND SUMERIANS

The Babylonians and Sumerians who lived in Mesopotamia during ancient times (c. 5400 BC) are credited with the earliest known observations of the Aries constellation. They associated this constellation with the cycles that were crucial to their society. Aries was commonly linked to the equinox. This marked the onset of spring and the beginning of their year. This event held great importance for their pursuits as it marked the commencement of the planting season. This was a time when they could sow crops with anticipation of a fruitful harvest, in due course. Consequently Aries became closely intertwined with rebirth and thus marked a new beginning for farming activities.

ANCIENT EGYPTIANS

The ancient Egyptians had an understanding of Aries, which played a key role in their belief systems and mythologies. Aries held a place in their worldview closely associated with the revered deity Amon Ra. Amon Ra, the powerful sun god was often depicted with the distinct curved horns of a ram. These horns were not just symbolic. This represented the connection between Amon Ra and the constellation Aries. The Egyptians saw Aries as an embodiment of power and the life giving force of the sun. The ram, symbolizing strength and protection, was considered a manifestation of Amon Ras' might. The image of the ram adorned temples, amulets and tombs—acting as both guardian and symbol of resilience.

Interestingly the ancient Egyptians approached astronomy differently from how we classify constellations in astronomy. Instead individual stars and groups of stars were linked to gods, legends and cosmic events. The stars, within the region we now know as Aries, were part of a tapestry that played a role in Egyptian religious and astronomical practices. This interconnected network of stars and their celestial narratives contributed to the mystical worldview of the Egyptians blurring the line between the earthly realm and the divine through the wonders of the night sky.

ANCIENT GREEKS

According to Greek mythology Aries is often linked to the captivating tale of the Golden Fleece and the adventures of Jason and the Argonauts. The story revolves around a ram adorned with a fleece that Jason and his crew eagerly pursued. This ram had been sent by Hermes and Athena to rescue Phrixus and Helle who were facing persecution from their stepmother. As a gesture of gratitude Phrixus sacrificed the ram upon reaching Colchis hanging its fleece on a tree as a symbol of appreciation. The Golden Fleece became an emblem of power and authority.

Furthermore Ares (the equivalent of the god Mars) known as the god of war in Greek mythology is often associated with the assertive and energetic qualities attributed to individuals born under the sign of Aries.

OTHER CULTURES

Various other cultures, such as the Persians and Indians had their own interpretations of Aries within their unique mythologies and knowledge of stars. These interpretations often touched upon themes of fertility, rejuvenation and seasonal transitions.

Overall the historical origins of the Aries constellation have deep roots, in various observations and interpretations made by civilizations. Whether seen as a symbol of renewal or associated with quests or divine protection Aries has carried diverse meanings across cultures enriching its celestial legacy in our night sky. To sum it up, ancient mythologies featuring Aries frequently symbolize courage, renewal and divine intervention. These mythical connections continue to infuse depth and symbolism into our understanding of Aries today.

EVOLUTION OF "ARIES"

Over time our perception and understanding of Aries in astrology has undergone many changes. Ancient civilizations primarily linked this sign with symbolism and mythology. However in modern astrology there has been a shift, towards psychological interpretations focusing on personality traits. Let's explore some key points that highlight this evolution.

Ancient Interpretations

In ancient times civilizations such as the Babylonians, Greeks and Egyptians associated Aries with cycles, mythical narratives and symbols of divinity. They emphasized its significance in terms of renewal and fertility.

Modern Astrology

Modern astrology offers insights into compatibility with zodiac signs as well as guidance regarding careers and relationship dynamics. This allows individuals to gain an understanding of themselves and make choices in their lives. In modern astrology Aries is considered one of the twelve zodiac signs that represent various personality traits and characteristics. Contemporary astrology delves into the aspects related to individuals born under the sign of Aries. It explores their strengths, weaknesses and potential life paths while emphasizing self awareness and personal growth.

To summarize, our understanding of Aries in astrology has transformed from symbolism to a modern perspective focused on psychology. While courage and initiative remain integral to its representation, contemporary astrology provides individuals with tools for self discovery and personal development in today's world.

HISTORICAL EVENTS

Throughout history many significant events have taken place during the season of Aries. The Aries zodiac sign is associated with qualities, like courage, initiative and leadership. Here are a few noteworthy historical events that occurred during this time and their possible astrological connections.

- **The American Revolution (1775 1783)**; The American Revolution, which saw the signing of the Declaration of Independence, on July 4 1776 took place during the Aries season. This period reflects the pioneering spirit of Aries as American colonists fought for their independence.
- **Apollo 11 Moon Landing (1969)**; The iconic Apollo 11 mission, where astronauts Neil Armstrong and Buzz Aldrin became the first humans to walk on the moon on July 20 1969 aligns with the Aries characteristic of pushing boundaries and venturing into territories.
- **The Fall of the Berlin Wall (1989)**; The fall of the Berlin Wall began on November 9 1989 leading to the reunification of East and West Germany. This event embodies the Aries trait of breaking barriers. Taking actions that bring about transformative change.

Historical figures

Throughout history there have been numerous figures born under the Aries zodiac sign who have left a lasting impact. Let's explore a few examples.

- **Leonardo da Vinci (April 15 1452)**; Leonardo da Vinci, a Renaissance man was born under the Aries sign. Made significant contributions to the fields of art, science and engineering. His genius and pioneering spirit truly embodied the qualities associated with Aries.
- **Thomas Jefferson (April 13 1743)**; Thomas Jefferson, one of the Founding Fathers of the United States and the principal author of the Declaration of Independence, leadership and determination that are often associated with Aries within the context of American history.
- **Maya Angelou (April 4 1928)**; Maya Angelou, a poet and civil rights activist born under Aries fearlessly used her voice to inspire and uplift others. Her assertiveness embodies one of the defining traits attributed to individuals born under this sign.

In conclusion we have delved into a captivating collection of tales and historical significance linked to Aries – a ram – throughout this chapter. From the search for the Golden Fleece to Amun Ra's symbolism Aries has stood as an emblem of bravery, rejuvenation and pioneering spirit across human history. These stories and mythologies have played a role in shaping this zodiac sign's enduring heritage.

Aries' impact is not limited to stories; it extends into the world of astrology today. The essential qualities of Aries –

bravery, leadership and a vibrant passion for life – still hold relevance in helping individuals understand themselves and navigate the complexities of the era. Aries guides us in embracing starts taking daring steps and connecting with our warriors.

For those interested in exploring the history and mythology of Aries here is a curated collection of sources ancient texts and contemporary writings;

- **"The Almagest"** by Claudius Ptolemy; An ancient text that offers valuable insights into the depiction and explanation of the Aries constellation's celestial significance.
- **"The Golden Fleece"** by Robert Graves; A literary journey delving into the legendary quest for the Golden Fleece and its connection to Aries in Greek mythology.
- **"The Oxford Guide to Classical Mythology**, in the Arts 1300 1990s" edited by Jane Davidson Reid; An reference work that provides perspectives on how Aries and other zodiac signs have influenced art, literature and culture throughout history.
- **"Astrology; Unraveling the Birth Chart"** written by Kevin Burk is a handbook that delves into the astrological dimensions of Aries and the complete zodiac providing valuable insights into its ongoing importance in modern astrology.

These references provide an, in depth comprehension of the captivating past, mythology and astrological implications associated with Aries.

CHAPTER 2:
LOVE & COMPATIBILITY

In the tapestry of the zodiac we welcome you into the captivating world of Aries individuals and their experiences, with love and compatibility. Exploring their dynamic nature we uncover their unique approach to romantic relationships. All this plus how they connect with zodiac signs. Join us as we navigate through Aries multifaceted love life and uncover the secrets of their compatibility. Whether you're an Aries seeking self discovery or looking to understand Aries in love, this chapter promises to be an enlightening journey.

ARIES APPROACH TO LOVE

Aries individuals embrace their qualities and fiery personality traits when it comes to matters of the heart. Here's a closer look at how.

- **Passionate and Intense**; Aries is renowned for its passion. When they fall in love they do so with enthusiasm and intensity. When it comes to romance, Aries individuals possess an intense passion. They are unafraid to openly express their feelings.
- **Fearless Pursuit**; Aries individuals have an inclination towards leadership. They don't hesitate when it comes to pursuing someone they are interested in. They enjoy the excitement of chasing after someone. For them they take pleasure in being the initiator who makes the first moves in a relationship.
- **Spontaneity and Adventure**; Aries thrives on excitement and adventure which also reflects in their approach to love. They are spontaneous by nature. They take delight in surprising their partners with outings, grand gestures and thrilling escapades. Routine and predictability simply don't fit into their love vocabulary.
- **Independence and Freedom**; Aries highly values their independence. As such they expect the same level of freedom from their partner. They need room to pursue their passions without feeling tied down. In a relationship they look for a partner who can match their lifestyle filled with activity.
- **Fiercely Loyal**; While Aries may enjoy seeking out experiences once they commit to a relationship they

display loyalty. In turn they stand firmly by their partner's side through thick and thin, always protective of those they love.
- **Direct Communication**; A known among Aries individuals is their directness, in communication. They prefer straightforwardness without beating around the bush or playing games. They value honesty and expect their partner to do the same. They don't enjoy playing mind games in relationships, preferring honest conversations, about their feelings and expectations.
- **Quick to Forgive;** Aries spontaneous nature can sometimes lead to conflicts or disagreements within a relationship. However they are quick to forgive and move forward from disputes as they don't hold grudges. Their ability to bounce back from disagreements with optimism is a characteristic.
- **Craving Challenges**; Aries individuals thrive when faced with challenges and this extends to their love life. They may seek partners who intellectually and emotionally stimulate them, keeping the relationship dynamic and exciting.
- **Physical Intimacy**; Physical attraction and intimacy are crucial for Aries in a relationship. They are lovers who enjoy expressing their emotions, desiring a partner who shares their enthusiasm for physical connection.

In conclusion Aries approaches love and romance with passion, intensity and an unwavering pursuit of excitement. Their direct communication style, loyalty and thirst for adventure make them captivating partners. However it's important to remember that each individual is unique so while these traits generally apply to Aries individuals, the specifics of how they approach love may vary from person to person.

COMPATIBILITY WITH OTHER ZODIAC SIGNS

When it comes to astrology compatibility is a key concept to consider. The compatibility between Aries individuals and other zodiac signs depends on elements, including the qualities of each partner and the dynamics of their relationship. Here's an overview of how Aries tends to interact with other zodiac signs.

ARIES AND ARIES

- Compatibility; A connection between two Aries individuals can be quite thrilling because of their shared sense of adventure and vitality. They truly understand each other's desire for freedom. As such they can inspire one another in many ways.
- Challenges; However there might be some challenges arising from both partners being strong willed and competitive. Power struggles or conflicts may occasionally occur. For this relationship to flourish it is crucial for them to find a common ground through compromise and effective communication.

ARIES AND TAURUS

- Compatibility; A pairing of an Aries and a Taurus can be intriguing due to their differences. While

Aries brings excitement and spontaneity. Taurus offers stability and grounding. Their contrasting qualities have the potential to complement one another effectively.
- Challenges; Nevertheless the impulsive nature of Aries might clash with the need for security and routine that Taurus seeks. To make this relationship work harmoniously, patience and understanding play important roles.

ARIES AND GEMINI

- Compatibility; When it comes to an Aries and Gemini pairing you'll find a love for stimulation, communication and social activities. Engaging conversations are likely as they both enjoy exploring varied concepts.
- Challenges; However at times Gemini's indecisiveness may test the patience of an action oriented Aries partner. Similarly Gemini might perceive Aries as being impulsive. Striking a balance between excitement and stability becomes essential in maintaining harmony in this relationship.

ARIES AND CANCER

- Compatibility; Although Aries and Cancer may have their differences they can actually complement each other well. Aries' energetic nature can help Cancer break out of their shell. Meanwhile Cancer's nurturing qualities can offer support to Aries.
- Challenges; However it's important for Aries to be mindful of how their directness may hurt Cancers

feelings. Likewise Aries should take care not to misunderstand or overlook the sensitivity that Cancer possesses. Effective communication and empathy are essential in navigating these challenges.

ARIES AND LEO

- Compatibility; When it comes to Aries and Leo they share a passion for life along with an adventurous spirit. Their relationship tends to be filled with excitement. This creates a fiery quality.
- Challenges; Both signs have a tendency towards dominance and driven behavior, which can sometimes lead to power struggles between them. Learning how to share the spotlight and avoiding conflicts fueled by ego is crucial in maintaining harmony.

ARIES AND VIRGO

- Compatibility; In the case of Aries and Virgo there is a dynamic at play. Aries has the ability to inspire Virgo to embrace spontaneity and adventure. Meanwhile Virgo brings practicality and organization into the mix – effectively balancing one another.
- Challenges; However it's worth noting that Aries impulsive nature might occasionally clash with Virgo's preference for orderliness. Additionally due to Virgo's tendencies there is a possibility that they could unintentionally undermine Aries self confidence. Patience, alongside acceptance are attributes needed in addressing these challenges effectively.

ARIES AND LIBRA

- Compatibility; Aries and Libra go well together because Aries is action oriented while Libra values harmony and balance. They can enjoy a loving life together.
- Challenges; Aries may sometimes find Libra hesitant in decision making. Similarly Libra might perceive Aries as being impulsive. It's important for them to find ground and be willing to compromise.

ARIES AND SCORPIO

- Compatibility; Aries and Scorpio share an intense connection. They have a physical bond often displaying unwavering loyalty towards each other.

- Challenges; Both signs can be stubborn and possessive leading to power struggles. Building trust through communication is crucial for maintaining a happy relationship.

ARIES AND SAGITTARIUS

- Compatibility; Aries and Sagittarius are both individuals who cherish their freedom. Together they delight in exploring life's wonders based on shared interests.
- Challenges; Their mutual love for independence may occasionally cause conflicts. However they can usually find ways to compromise without dampening their enthusiasm.

ARIES AND CAPRICORN

- Compatibility; Aries ambitious nature often aligns well with Capricorn's drive for success in life. They can greatly motivate each other to achieve their goals together.
- Challenges; Aries impatience may not always align with Capricorn's practical approach. It is important for them to find a common ground between taking calculated risks and making decisions.

ARIES AND AQUARIUS

- Compatibility; Aries and Aquarius value individuality and innovation which can lead to a fulfilling connection. They both enjoy embarking on new adventures.

- Challenges; Aries spontaneous nature may sometimes clash with Aquarius' desire for unpredictability. Meanwhile Aquarius' tendency to be detached might pose a challenge for Aries. Open communication plays an important role in overcoming these obstacles.

ARIES AND PISCES

- Compatibility; Aries and Pisces have differences that can either complement or create conflicts, within their relationship. The strength of Aries combined with the sensitivity of Pisces can foster a nurturing dynamic.
- Challenges; Aries straightforwardness may unintentionally hurt the feelings of Pisces. Meanwhile, the dreamy nature of Pisces could confuse Aries. Building trust and emotional understanding are important aspects for their relationship to thrive.

Note that it's important to keep in mind that while astrology can offer insights into compatibility factors such as personality, life experiences and communication skills play a role in determining the success of a relationship. Many successful relationships thrive between individuals with energies indicating that astrological signs alone do not determine compatibility.

TIPS FOR DATING AND NURTURING RELATIONSHIPS WITH ARIES

Dating and nurturing relationships with Aries individuals can be an fulfilling experience. However it's essential to understand their qualities and needs. Whether you're a man or a woman here are some tips for establishing and sustaining a bond with an Aries.

TIPS FOR MEN DATING ARIES WOMEN

- **Confidence is Key**; Aries women are drawn to confidence and assertiveness. Display confidence by making decisive actions and choices.
- **Respect Their Independence**; Aries women highly value their independence and freedom. Encourage their pursuits and passions while also maintaining your own interests and independence.
- **Embrace Adventure**; Aries women thrive on excitement and spontaneity. Plan thrilling dates that keep the relationship vibrant and dynamic.
- **Honesty and Transparency**; Aries women value honesty and straightforwardness. It's important to communicate your feelings and intentions to establish trust.
- **Show Support**; Aries women are ambitious and driven. Show support for their goals and dreams. Be their cheerleader during challenging times.

TIPS FOR WOMEN DATING ARIES MEN

- **Respect Their Need for Independence**; Aries men highly value their independence. Give them

space to pursue their interests without overwhelming them with attention.
- **Appreciate Their Initiatives**; Aries men are leaders and initiators. Appreciate their efforts in planning dates and making decisions.
- **Be Confident and Self Assured**; Aries men are attracted to partners who exude confidence. Believe in yourself and showcase your abilities. Overall this will make you more attractive to them.
- **Engage in Physical Activities**; Aries men enjoy being active and participating in physical activities. Join them in sports, workouts or outdoor adventures to bond over shared enthusiasm.
- **Communicate Openly**; Aries men appreciate communication. If you have any concerns or desires express them clearly as they prefer honesty and straightforwardness.

GENERAL TIPS FOR DATING AND RELATIONSHIPS WITH ARIES

- **Embrace Spontaneity**; Aries individuals thrive on spontaneity and excitement. Be open, to impromptu plans or adventures that keep the relationship alive.
- **Practice Patience**; Aries people tend to act on impulse, which can occasionally lead to disagreements. It's important to practice patience and find compromises in order to resolve conflicts.
- **Finding a balance is key**; Strive to strike a balance, between giving them space for independence and nurturing your bond with them. Encourage their growth while cherishing the connection you share.

- **Celebrate their accomplishments**; Aries individuals are highly motivated by success. Take the time to celebrate their achievements, even the small ones as it will bring them happiness.
- **Don't forget about your interests**; While nurturing the relationship remember to maintain your passions and pursuits. Aries individuals appreciate partners who have their own hobbies and goals.
- **Respect boundaries**; Aries individuals have boundaries so it's crucial to respect their limits. Open communication about your boundaries will contribute to creating a respectful partnership.

Remember that astrology provides insights. Individual personalities and compatibility are influenced by various factors beyond zodiac signs. Building a relationship with an Aries individual requires understanding, compromise and open communication. Just like any other relationship.

In conclusion of the chapter "Love & Compatibility " we have explored the passionate nature of Aries individuals when it comes to matters of the heart.

From the fearless way they approach love and romance to their intense energy, individuals born under the sign of Aries bring a dynamic and thrilling presence to their relationships.

We have delved into the complexities of Aries compatibility, with zodiac signs discovering the chemistry and challenges that arise when an Aries pairs up with different celestial counterparts. Whether they find harmony with Fire signs, engage in stimulating connections with Air signs or navigate the depths of emotional intimacy with Water signs, Aries romantic journey is marked by excitement, personal growth and occasional clashes of will.

As we wrap up this chapter one thing remains crystal clear; Aries individuals approach love and relationships with unwavering courage and boundless enthusiasm. They are determined to conquer any challenges that come their way and are eager to experience the thrill of connection.

CHAPTER 3: FRIENDS AND FAMILY

This chapter explores the loyalty and leadership that Aries brings to their friendships well as the profound impact they have on family dynamics. With their inclination for leadership and fierce protectiveness Aries individuals establish connections, inspire those around them and navigate challenges in their pursuit of harmonious relationships.

Here we delve into the qualities and challenges that arise for Aries individuals as they balance their assertive caring nature in both friendships and family relationships. Whether you are an Aries seeking an understanding of your role in these relationships or a curious reader interested in gaining insight into the world of Aries connections, this chapter promises an enlightening journey through the intricate bonds and dynamics within friends and family.

ARIES AS A FRIEND

Being friends with an Aries is an invigorating experience full of vibrancy. Aries friends possess a combination of qualities that make them loyal and exhilarating companions. Here's what you can expect when befriending an Aries;

- **Loyalty and Reliability**; Aries friends display loyalty and reliability. When Aries individuals commit to a friendship they are unwavering in their loyalty and support. You can always count on them to have your back no matter the circumstances.
- **Spontaneity**; One remarkable quality of Aries friends is their spontaneous spirit. They have a thrilling nature that makes every experience exciting and new. With them there's never a dull moment.
- **Leading**; Aries friends naturally take charge to lead the way. They are proactive, in planning outings, gatherings and activities. Their ability to rally the group and make things happen is truly admirable.
- **Honesty**; Honesty is highly valued by Aries individuals when it comes to friendships. They appreciate direct communication from their friends without any sugar coating. In return they expect the same level of transparency.

- **Supportive**; Supporting your dreams and ambitions is something Aries friends excel at. They are incredibly supportive. They will motivate you to reach your goals while helping you overcome obstacles along the way.
- **Enthusiasm**; Aries friends bring an enthusiastic vibe wherever they go. Their infectious energy adds excitement to gatherings inspiring others to join in on the fun.
- **Solutions focused**; Problem solving comes naturally to Aries individuals. Whenever their friends face challenges or difficulties they quickly offer solutions with a helping hand.
- **Forgiving**; Forgiveness is a virtue that Aries' friends possess. They have a nature that allows them to solve conflicts or misunderstandings, for the sake of maintaining strong friendships. Aries ' friends may get angry quickly. But they are just as quick to forgive and move on from disagreements. They don't hold grudges and prefer to maintain a friendship.
- **Protective Nature**; Aries friends have an instinct to protect their loved ones and will go to great lengths to ensure their safety and well being.
- **Independence and Freedom**; Aries' friends value their independence and expect their friends to respect their need for personal space and freedom. They appreciate friends who support their pursuits.

While Aries friends bring qualities into your life it's important to remember that their assertiveness and occasional impatience can lead to conflicts. However these conflicts are usually short lived as Aries forgiving nature ensures that friendships remain strong.

In conclusion, having an Aries friend means having an adventurous and supportive companion by your side. Their dynamic personality and zest for life can add excitement and vitality to your friendship creating a memorable connection.

ARIES IN FAMILY DYNAMICS

Aries individuals bring their unique qualities and characteristics into family dynamics influencing the atmosphere within the household as well as interactions, among family members. Understanding the role of Aries in family life can provide key insights into how they contribute, face challenges and shape family dynamics.

- **Natural Leaders**; Aries individuals often step into leadership positions within their families. They are proactive and assertive, taking charge of decision making and problem solving. They may naturally gravitate towards being the spokesperson for the family or organizing family events.
- **Protectors and Defenders**; Aries individuals possess an instinct to protect especially when it comes to their loved ones. They are fiercely loyal and will stand up for their family members if they perceive any threat or injustice.
- **Independence and Autonomy**; Aries highly value their independence and autonomy which can sometimes create conflicts within family dynamics. They may resist controlling or restrictive family settings. Overall they prefer to have a certain level of personal freedom.

- **Sibling Rivalry**; Aries assertiveness and desire to excel may lead to rivalries with their brothers or sisters. While healthy competition can be beneficial it's important for parents to promote cooperation and teamwork among siblings.
- **Parenting Approach**; Aries parents tend to be energetic and actively involved in their children's lives. They encourage independence and self confidence from an early age nurturing a sense of empowerment in their kids.
- **Teaching Resilience**; Aries parents and family members demonstrate resilience by exemplifying courage when faced with challenges. They impart the belief that setbacks are opportunities for growth and learning experiences.
- **Conflict Resolution**; Although Aries family members may sometimes have tempers, their ability to forgive and move on swiftly contributes to maintaining a happy atmosphere. It is crucial for them to work on communication skills and conflict resolution techniques.
- **Celebrating Achievements;** Aries individuals take pride in acknowledging their families accomplishments and milestones. With enthusiasm they celebrate birthdays, graduations and other significant achievements making family gatherings truly memorable.
- **Spontaneous Adventures;** Aries family members infuse an element of spontaneity into their shared experiences. They welcome outings and adventures ensuring that family activities remain exciting and dynamic.

- **Supportive and Encouraging**; Aries family members provide unwavering support to their loved ones. They actively encourage family members to pursue their dreams and passions fostering a sense of self belief, within the unit.

Overall, within the dynamics of a family Aries assertiveness and protective nature contribute to creating a sense of security and empowerment among its members. While they may encounter challenges related to independence or conflicts at times. Overall their ability to forgive and move forward ensures the strength of bonds remains intact. Ultimately Aries brings an active presence to family life promoting growth, resilience and a strong sense of individuality, among family members.

CHALLENGES IN FRIENDSHIPS AND FAMILY

Although Aries individuals bring beneficial qualities to their friendships and family relationships they may also encounter certain challenges due to their assertive and dynamic nature. Here are some common difficulties they might face.

- **Spontaneity**; Aries individuals are known for their spontaneous nature. While this can lead to nice experiences it can also result in decisions or actions that may have negative consequences in both friendships and family relationships. Taking a moment to consider the potential outcomes can be beneficial.
- **Assertiveness vs. Aggression**; Sometimes Aries assertiveness can be mistaken for aggression, which

could lead to conflicts in both friendships and family dynamics. Learning how to balance their assertiveness with diplomacy and sensitivity can help them avoid misunderstandings.

- **Independence and Personal Space**; Aries values their independence and the need for space. Striking a balance between their desire for freedom and the expectations of relationships can be challenging, particularly if friends or family perceive them as distant or unavailable.
- **Impatience**; Aries individuals often prefer results. As such they may become impatient when things don't go according to plan or meet their expectations. Such impatience can put a strain on relationships both with friends and family, especially if they expect others to keep up with their pace.
- **Resolving Conflicts**; Aries individuals are not afraid to address conflicts. Their direct and sometimes confrontational communication style can be overwhelming, for others. Learning to approach conflicts with patience and empathy can lead to resolutions.
- **Balancing Priorities**; Aries individuals feel a sense of responsibility towards their family. Their active social lives can sometimes make it challenging to find a balance. Managing time effectively is important in order to fulfill family commitments while also nurturing friendships.
- **Competitiveness**; Aries competitive nature, in friendships with Aries or competitive family members can lead to rivalry and tension. Encouraging cooperation and celebrating each

other's successes is crucial in maintaining relationships.
- **Stubbornness**; Aries individuals tend to be stubborn when they believe they are right. This stubbornness can result in disagreements and conflicts within familial relationships. Learning to compromise and be open minded towards others perspectives is essential.
- **Forgiveness**; While Aries individuals may get angry quickly they also have the ability to forgive swiftly. However it's important to recognize that not everyone processes their emotions at the pace as them. Patience and understanding play a role, in resolving conflicts.
- **Burnout**; Aries' boundless energy levels have the potential to lead to exhaustion, which can impact their ability to maintain bonds with friends and family. It is important for them to recognize the value of self care and taking breaks when necessary in order to avoid burning out.

To sum it up, Aries individuals bring enthusiasm, leadership and loyalty into their friendships and family relationships. On the other hand they also face challenges related to acting on impulse and overly asserting themselves. By acknowledging these challenges and focusing on growth and effective communication Aries individuals can cultivate better connections with their loved ones.

In our exploration of "Aries; Friends And Family " we have delved into the dynamics that Aries individuals contribute to their friend circles and familial ties. Their unwavering loyalty, leadership qualities and passionate nature leave an impact on the lives of those they hold dear. However as with any aspect of life there is always room for improvement, maintenance and growth within these relationships. Here are some final tips to enhance, nurture and develop relationships.

ENHANCING RELATIONSHIPS

- **Embrace Patience**; Aries individuals tend to be impulsive and quick, in their actions. To enhance their relationships they can work on slowing down, actively listening to others perspectives and

considering the consequences before making decisions.
- **Improve Communication**; Although Aries tends to be direct, honing their communication skills can help them express their thoughts and feelings. Overall this will help in reducing misunderstandings and conflicts.
- **Embrace Flexibility**; Aries enthusiasm, for spontaneity is great. It's equally important to be adaptable to others schedules and preferences. Being flexible promotes interactions.

NURTURING RELATIONSHIPS

- **Quality Time**; Continue prioritizing quality time with friends and family. Regular get-togethers and meaningful conversations will help nurture connections.
- **Consistent Support**; Offering support and encouragement to loved ones ensures that relationships remain nurturing and reliable.
- **Respect Boundaries**; Show respect for others boundaries while also communicating your own. Healthy relationships are built on respect for space and independence.

DEVELOPING RELATIONSHIPS

- **Cultivate Empath**y; Aries individuals can benefit from cultivating empathy. Understanding others' emotions and perspectives fosters deeper connections.

- **Emphasize Cooperation**; Encourage cooperation, then competition in friendships and family dynamics. Collaborating strengthens bonds while minimizing conflicts.
- **Reflect and Learn**; Take time to reflect on interactions and relationships. Learning from both successes and challenges can lead to growth and stronger connections.

To sum up, Aries individuals have the potential to create friendships and maintain family relationships by practicing patience, effective communication and a willingness to adapt. By fostering these relationships with care and commitment Aries individuals will discover that their distinct attributes enrich the lives of their loved ones resulting in lasting and loving ways.

CHAPTER 4: CAREER AND AMBITIONS

This chapter uncovers the ambitious nature of Aries individuals in their financial endeavors. It explores how Aries approaches their career path, goals and the strategies they employ to achieve success. Here we also delve into the strengths and challenges that Aries faces on their journey. From their ability to lead to their inclination for decision making, we examine what sets them apart. Whether you're an Aries seeking an understanding of your career and financial aspirations or a curious reader interested in gaining insights into how Aries thinks about money. This chapter offers an exploration of how Aries pursues success, stability and prosperity.

ARIES CAREER PREFERENCES AND PROFESSIONAL GOALS

Aries individuals are known for being dynamic and ambitious which significantly shapes their career preferences and professional goals. Let's take a look at what drives and motivates them in the world of work.

- **Leadership Roles**; Aries individuals have an inclination towards leadership positions. They gravitate towards careers that allow them to take

charge, make decisions and guide others. They thrive when given authority roles such as managers or team leaders.
- **Solutions based**; Thriving in stimulating work environments is where Aries individuals shine. They find their energy through competition problem solving and conquering hurdles. Careers in sales, marketing and entrepreneurship hold an appeal for them. Aries people have a knack for solving problems. In addition they thrive in careers that demand thinking, adaptability and the ability to make decisions under pressure.
- **Independence**; Independence holds value to Aries individuals. They gravitate towards careers that allow them to work independently or grant them the freedom to make decisions and set goals. Pursuing freelancing opportunities consulting roles or venturing into entrepreneurship are paths for them.
- **Entrepreneurship**; The entrepreneurial spirit runs strong in Aries individuals. They embrace risks. Eagerly pursue ideas. Starting their businesses or working in startup environments aligns perfectly with their desire for independence and innovation.
- **Driven**; Being goal oriented is a defining trait of Aries individuals. They set targets for themselves. Tirelessly they work towards achieving them. Careers that offer milestones and avenues for growth hold allure.
- **Adventurous;** Aries adventurous nature often leads them towards professions that involve travel, exploration or physical challenges. Their inclinations draw them towards fields such as adventure sports, travel blogging or outdoor guiding.

- **Competitive**; Competition fuels the fire within Aries individuals, who relish being acknowledged for their accomplishments. Often gravitating towards careers, in sports, entertainment or fields where they can showcase their talents and receive recognition.
- **Continuous Learning**; Aries individuals have a thirst for knowledge and enjoy acquiring new skills. They might pursue careers in technology, research or fields where they can continually expand their expertise.
- **Making a Difference**; Many Aries individuals are driven by the desire to create an impact on the world. They may choose careers in activism, social justice or advocacy to channel their passion for change.

While an Aries individual's career preferences and professional aspirations are influenced by their traits and characteristics it's important to remember that individual personalities vary. Some Aries individuals may find fulfillment in careers aligned with these preferences while others may explore alternative paths. Ultimately Aries determination, energy and leadership skills make them valuable assets in endeavors where they can pave the way and achieve remarkable success.

ARIES STRENGTHS IN THE WORKPLACE

Aries individuals possess a set of strengths and qualities that propel them towards success, in the workplace. Notably, Aries individuals possess an assertive nature that sets them apart as contributors. Let's explore some strengths that contribute to their success, in careers;

- **Leadership Skills**; Aries has a talent for leadership exhibiting confidence and taking charge of situations. Their ability to inspire and guide others proves valuable in leadership positions
- **Proactive Approach**; Aries individuals are known for their nature, always eager to take the initiative rather than waiting for instructions. This quality makes them efficient workers.
- **Unyielding Determination**; Aries is renowned for their determination. Once they set their sights on a goal they pursue it relentlessly often overcoming obstacles through willpower.
- **Fearlessness**; Aries individuals fearlessly embrace risks and challenges. They approach situations with courage. Eagerly seize opportunities that others may

shy away from. This fearlessness often leads to innovation and groundbreaking achievements.

- **Competitive Spirit**; Aries thrives on competition viewing challenges as opportunities to demonstrate their abilities and excel. Their competitive drive propels them to consistently improve themselves and surpass expectations.
- **Swift Decision Making**; Aries individuals possess the ability to make decisions under high pressure circumstances. Their decisive nature enables them to navigate situations. The skill of thinking is valuable, in fast paced work environments.
- **Problem Solving Abilities**; Aries demonstrates intellect and problem solving skills. They excel at analyzing issues, identifying solutions and implementing them.
- **Independence**; Aries highly values their independence. Thrives in situations where they can work autonomously. They are self motivated, require supervision and can handle tasks and projects independently.
- **Productive**; Aries individuals possess levels of energy and productivity. They have a drive to efficiently accomplish tasks without getting fatigued.
- **Innovation**; Aries' innovative mindset and willingness to explore ideas contribute significantly to their success. They are open to experimenting with new approaches and finding creative solutions when faced with challenges.
- **Resilience**; Aries individuals quickly bounce back from setbacks. They view failures as opportunities for growth remaining undeterred by career obstacles.

- **Charisma**; Many Aries individuals possess a personality that enables them to communicate effectively and negotiate skillfully. Their ability to influence others makes them valuable in many professions.
- **Passion**; Aries is deeply passionate about their work. Their enthusiasm and dedication inspire both themselves and their colleagues to strive for excellence.
- **Time Management**; Aries individuals are adept at managing their time. They prioritize their tasks. Maintain an approach ensuring that they meet deadlines and achieve their goals.
- **Being a team player**; Although Aries individuals enjoy taking on leadership roles they also excel as team players. Their competitive spirit drives them to collaborate with others in order to accomplish shared objectives.

These strengths, combined with Aries innate determination and assertiveness make them valuable assets, in the workplace. They thrive in positions that require leadership, innovation and the ability to tackle challenges head on. Aries individuals are highly motivated to achieve success and their dynamic work approach often leads to accomplishments in their careers.

CHALLENGES FACED BY ARIES AND STRATEGIES TO OVERCOME THEM

While Aries individuals possess strengths that can propel them towards career success they also face specific challenges due to their assertive and dynamic nature. Understanding these challenges and implementing strategies to overcome them can result in a fulfilling and well balanced professional life;

Impulsivity

- Challenge; At times Aries individuals may act impulsively by making decisions without considering the potential consequences.
- Strategy; Before making decisions take a moment for reflection. Carefully evaluate all available information. Seek input from trusted colleagues or mentors to ensure an informed choice.

Impatience

- Challenge; Aries impatience can sometimes lead to frustration when they don't see results or when their colleagues work at a pace.
- Strategy; It's important for Aries to practice patience and understand that not all projects or processes will deliver outcomes. Setting expectations and focusing on progress is key.

Conflict Resolution

- Challenge; Aries individuals have a tendency to be direct and confrontational which can create conflicts with their colleagues or superiors.
- Strategy; Developing conflict resolution skills involves listening to others perspectives and finding common ground. Diplomacy and tact are valuable in maintaining working relationships.

Burnout

- Challenge; Aries high energy levels can sometimes lead to burnout if they neglect self care.
- Strategy; Prioritizing self care is essential for Aries. Incorporating breaks, exercise and relaxation techniques into their routine helps recharge their energy levels and sustain long term productivity.

Balancing Independence and Teamwork

- Challenge; While independence is important for Aries they also need to work within teams.
- Strategy; Embracing collaboration is crucial, for Aries. Recognizing the strengths of colleagues and understanding that teamwork often leads to outcomes and personal growth is vital.

Delegation

- Challenge; Delegating tasks may be challenging for Aries as they prefer handling everything themselves.
- Strategy; Aries individuals should consider the benefits of delegation. Trusting others with tasks allows them to focus on responsibilities while fostering a sense of teamwork. Be patient, in advancing your career;

Rushing

- Challenge; Aries strong desire to quickly climb the ladder may lead to frustration if promotions or opportunities do not materialize swiftly as expected.
- Strategy; Establish career objectives. Work steadily towards achieving them. Understand that career growth often requires patience and continuous development of skills.

Embrace diplomacy

- Challenge; Aries straightforwardness may sometimes be perceived as abrupt or confrontational in environments.
- Strategy; Practice the art of diplomacy by choosing your words and considering the impact your communication may have. Foster an atmosphere of respect and cooperation.

Recognize the value of experience

- Challenge; Aries may underestimate the importance of experience becoming overly focused on pursuing challenges.
- Strategy; Acknowledge the wisdom that comes with experience and seek guidance from professionals. By combining enthusiasm with experience you can achieve success.

Maintain a work life balance

- Challenge; Aries dedication to their careers can occasionally disrupt their work life balance.
- Strategy; Prioritize maintaining a work life balance by setting boundaries and making time for family, relaxation and personal interests.

Introspection and awareness ultimately leads to improved performance. By acknowledging and addressing these obstacles individuals born under the zodiac sign Aries can effectively utilize their strengths. As such they can navigate their careers, with success and fulfillment. Overcoming these challenges can result in a sustainable professional journey.

In this chapter we have discovered the dynamic nature of Aries individuals as they pursue their professional goals and financial aspirations. Their unwavering determination, inherent leadership qualities and competitive spirit make them formidable contenders in the realms of career and finance.

We have also explored the difficulties they encounter such as impulsiveness and impatience along with strategies to overcome them. The path that Aries individuals embark upon in terms of their career and finances is characterized by enthusiasm, ambition as a pursuit of personal success both financially and professionally.

As we bring this chapter to a close it becomes evident that individuals born under Aries are fueled by a desire to accomplish their objectives, ascend the career ladder and secure their future. Their dynamic approach coupled with a willingness to adapt and grow, positions them for excellence.

CHAPTER 5:
SELF-IMPROVEMENT

With their ambitious nature Aries are always motivated to refine their strengths, address weaknesses and strive for achievements. This chapter delves into the path of self improvement for Aries individuals providing guidance and exercises tailored to their unique personality traits. Whether you're an Aries seeking growth or a curious reader intrigued by the world of the Ram, this chapter guarantees an inspiring exploration of the relentless pursuit of self improvement and excellence.

EMBRACING ARIES STRENGTHS AND OVERCOMING WEAKNESSES

Like every zodiac sign, Aries individuals possess a unique set of strengths and weaknesses. To maximize their potential for success and personal growth Aries can leverage their strengths while working on overcoming weaknesses. Here's a guide on how to accomplish that.

UTILIZING STRENGTHS;

- **Leadership Skills**; Embrace leadership roles, in both personal and professional spheres. Utilize your ability to inspire others and provide guidance to foster change.
- **Taking Initiative**; Keep embracing challenges by taking initiative and actively seeking out projects. Your ability to take initiative and motivate yourself sets you apart and contributes to your success.
- **Determination**; Focus your determination, on setting goals and staying committed to achieving them. Your unwavering dedication is an asset.
- **Fearlessness**; Embrace calculated risks. View them as opportunities for growth and innovation. Your willingness to take risks can lead to breakthroughs.
- **Competitive Spirit**; Use your competitive nature as motivation to set professional benchmarks. Let competition drive you towards self improvement.

OVERCOMING WEAKNESSES

- **Impulsivity**; Practice mindfulness and take a moment to pause before taking action. Developing patience will help you make better decisions.
- **Impatience**; Cultivate patience by setting timelines and understanding that success often takes time and perseverance. Be patient in your career advancement by setting goals and keeping track of your progress. Remember that climbing the career ladder often requires time and experience.
- **Conflict Resolution**; Work on improving your diplomacy skills and actively listening to others during conflicts. Approach disagreements with empathy for seeking common ground.
- **Burnout**; Prioritize self care to prevent burnout. Schedule regular breaks, engage in hobbies. Overall maintain a work life balance.
- **Balancing Independence and Teamwork**; Embrace collaboration with colleagues recognizing their strengths while acknowledging the benefits of teamwork for growth and better outcomes.
- **Delegation**; Learn to trust others capabilities by delegating tasks within your team or organization allowing yourself more time for responsibilities.
- **Practice diplomacy**; Choose your words and consider how they will impact others. Create an atmosphere of respect and collaboration through communication.
- **Recognize the value of experience**; Seek guidance from professionals. Combining enthusiasm with wisdom gained from experience can lead to more success.

- **Set boundaries**; Prioritize maintaining a work life balance by setting boundaries and making time for relaxation, family and personal interests. A balanced life contributes to overall well being and enhanced performance.

By embracing their strengths and actively working on improving their weaknesses Aries individuals can unlock their full potential. Overall they can achieve greater success in both personal and professional domains. Self awareness along with a commitment to growth plays an important role in thriving in all aspects of life.

PERSONAL DEVELOPMENT

Aries individuals are known for their ambition which makes personal growth an essential part of their journey. To evolve and flourish Aries can focus on areas of self improvement while harnessing their strengths. Here's a personalized guide to help Aries individuals grow.

- **Self Reflection**; Take the time to reflect on yourself and gain an understanding of your strengths, weaknesses and motivations. Having self awareness is crucial for growth and development.
- **Cultivating Patience**; Develop patience by practicing mindfulness and recognizing that not everything happens instantly. Embracing patience allows you to make better decisions and effectively navigate challenges.
- **Emotional Understanding**; Nurture your intelligence by listening to others. Empathize with their feelings and understand the impact your words and actions have on those around you.
- **Resolving Conflicts**; Work on your skills. Learn effective conflict resolution strategies. Address conflicts with empathy, patience and the intention of finding solutions.
- **Effective Time Management;** Improve your time management skills to maintain a balance in your lifestyle. Prioritize. Allocate time for work, personal life and self care to avoid burnout.
- **Fostering Empathy**; Cultivate empathy as it helps you better understand others and connect with them on a level. Individuals who are empathetic often have happier relationships and can inspire others more effectively.

- **Embracing Collaboration**; Recognize the value of collaboration and teamwork by embracing the input of others in generating insights and ideas. Balancing independence with collaboration leads to improved outcomes.
- **Lead with Compassion;** Apply your leadership skills with compassion and empathy taking into consideration the needs and emotions of others. Guide them on their journeys.

By dedicating yourself to growth and development in these aspects individuals born under the sign of Aries can tap into their strengths and become even more dynamic, understanding and successful human beings. Remember that personal growth is a process and every step you take contributes to a meaningful and purposeful life.

To recap, in this chapter we have delved into the path of growth that defines individuals born under the sign of Aries. With their determination, natural leadership qualities and ambitious nature Aries individuals possess huge potential for self improvement.

Throughout this chapter we have discussed a variety of exercises and practices tailored specifically to address both the strengths and challenges to Aries. These include techniques, strategies and exercises. By embracing these, Aries individuals can fully utilize their qualities while also addressing areas that may require further development.

The future holds endless possibilities for individuals born under the sign of Aries.

Their unwavering pursuit of excellence coupled with their dedication to self improvement positions them for a future marked by accomplishment, satisfaction and personal development. As they further refine their leadership abilities, foster connections with others and navigate challenges with skillfulness, they have the potential to unlock their fullest capabilities. In turn they can make a lasting impact on the world around them.

Ultimately, the journey of self improvement is an endless adventure and Aries individuals possess the qualities to embark on this path with eagerness, resilience and a vibrant spirit. As they continue to grow and evolve they are bound to inspire those in their presence and attain lasting success.

CHAPTER 6: ARIES IN THE YEAR AHEAD

Welcome to a fresh new chapter! Here we will delve into how the celestial forces will shape the experiences, aspirations and obstacles that Aries individuals may encounter in the year ahead. Known for their assertive nature as the sign of the zodiac Aries is always ready to embrace new adventures and face challenges head on. Within this chapter we will dive into the influence of events on Aries love life, career path, financial matters, health, personal growth and much more. By highlighting dates and time periods of importance our aim is to provide insights and guidance that will assist you in navigating through these currents.

The year ahead presents a tapestry woven with opportunities for growth, self reflection and transformation. So buckle up for this celestial journey to uncover what lies ahead for you under the stars in the coming year.

HOROSCOPE GUIDE FOR ARIES

The year ahead has much in store for Aries. Here is a closer look of what to expect.

- **January - March (Aries Season);** The year starts off with your season Aries! It's a time to set goals and take the lead, in all aspects of life. Focus on your aspirations. You'll see your determination bear fruit.

- **April - June;** During this period relationships and partnerships become important. Be open to collaborating and finding common ground. Balancing assertiveness with diplomacy will be key.
- **July - September;** Mid year brings many opportunities for career growth and recognition. Your leadership abilities will flourish. You may receive deserved praise or even promotions.
- **October - December;** As the year comes to a close it's a moment to reflect on your objectives. Pay attention to budgeting and term financial planning for securing your future.

KEY THEMES FOR THE YEAR

- **Career Advancement**; This year presents opportunities for reaching new heights in your journey through ambition and determination. Embrace leadership roles, set goals and seize growth prospects.
- **Relationship Dynamics**; Give importance to both professional relationships. Strive for a balance between assertiveness and empathy while seeking connections.
- **Financial Planning**; Take a look at your finances. Consider long term goals as you plan ahead. Responsible management of your finances and making investments will pave the way for a prosperous financial future.
- **Personal Growth**; Keep nurturing your growth and development. Cultivate patience, practice mindfulness and work on improving your skills in diplomacy and conflict resolution.
- **Exploration**; Fulfill your spirit by exploring horizons be it through travel learning new things or pursuing exciting hobbies.
- **Health and Wellbeing**; Make self care a priority. Maintain a balance between work and personal life. Regular exercise, relaxation techniques and a balanced diet are crucial for your well being.
- **Creativity and Innovation**; Allow your creativity to flow freely this year. Channel that energy into projects or ventures that showcase your talents.
- **Family and Home**; Strengthen the bonds with your family members while creating a nurturing home environment. Your leadership qualities can

serve as a source of support and inspiration for your loved ones.
- **Networking and Connections**; Expand your network by connecting with new and old connections. New friendships or partnerships may open up opportunities for you.

Remember that astrology provides guidance but doesn't determine your destiny entirely. Your choices and actions play a role in shaping the course of your life.

Embrace the opportunities and challenges that come your way with confidence and enthusiasm and you'll make the most of your year Aries!

ASTROLOGICAL INFLUENCES ON ARIES

Throughout the year Aries individuals, who are known for their assertive nature will be influenced by notable astrology events. These celestial happenings can shape their experiences, moods and opportunities. Here are some important astrological events and how they may impact Aries.

- **Aries Season (March 21. April 19);** During the period when the sun moves through your sign in the Aries season your energy and motivation reach their peak. It's a time for rejuvenation, self exploration and setting goals for the year.
- **Venus in Aries (February 20 to March 16) ;** When Venus, the planet associated with love and relationships transits through Aries it gives a boost to your life as well as social interactions. You may

feel more assertive in pursuing your desires and forming connections.

- **Mars Retrograde (periodic) ;** Mars is considered your ruling planet so its retrogrades can have an impact on you. During Mars retrograde periods you might experience a decrease in energy levels and assertiveness compared to times. This is an opportunity for reflection and practicing patience.
- **Full Moon (monthly);** Every month when the full moon appears it can bring about new emotions. It will shed light on your relationships and personal life. It's a moment to let go of what does not serve you and make adjustments, in different aspects of your life.
- **Arrival of a New Moon (monthly);** The arrival of a new moon each month signifies starts and opportunities to set intentions. As an Aries individual you can use these moments to initiate projects, embark on ventures or make changes in your life.
- **Mercury Retrograde (periodic) ;** Periodically during Mercury retrograde phases be cautious about communication and travel. It's advisable for Aries individuals to double check plans. Exercise care in their interactions during these periods to avoid misunderstandings.
- **Jupiter and Saturn (periodic);** Throughout the year pay attention to the movements of Jupiter and Saturn as they traverse zodiac signs. These transitions can have an impact on your long term goals and personal growth. They may present opportunities for expansion as discipline.

- **Eclipses (periodic);** The times of year when eclipses occur signify shifts in your life and will alter your perspective on things. Be prepared for events that may arise during these times and be open to uncovering truths about yourself or situations around you.
- **Retrograde of other Planets (periodic);** At times throughout the year keep an eye out for retrograde planets like Venus, Mars or Jupiter. These planetary retrogrades might prompt you to reassess relationships, career choices or personal beliefs that are important to you.
- **Solar and Lunar Eclipses (Twice a Year);** Aries individuals may experience noticeable effects during lunar and solar eclipses. These celestial events have the potential to bring about moments that motivate them to take action or make life decisions.

In conclusion Aries individuals are renowned for their dynamic personality traits. Being the sign of the zodiac they embody the essence of beginnings and fresh starts. Aries people are driven, enthusiastic and always prepared to embrace challenges. Their fearless approach to life often leads them to accomplishments and triumphs.

Remember that it's important to understand that astrology provides guidance and insights. Ultimately our actions and choices shape our destiny. Aries individuals can utilize celestial events, as tools, for self awareness and personal growth adapting to the changing energies in order to lead fulfilling and purposeful lives.

Looking ahead to the upcoming year, Aries individuals can utilize their energy and determination to pursue their goals and aspirations. This may involve setting intentions, refining their leadership abilities and directing their spirit towards positive endeavors. It is also crucial for Aries individuals to nurture their relationships as sometimes their spirited nature can lead to conflicts.

Overall the year ahead is a time for reaching new levels of success, while inspiring those around them with their fearlessness and adventurous spirit. Of course we wish you the very best

CHAPTER 7: FAMOUS ARIES PERSONALITIES

In this chapter we embark on a journey exploring the lives and accomplishments of some of the world's most famous individuals who were born under the zodiac sign of Aries. Aries individuals are well known for their assertive nature, which often drives them to achieve greatness. From actors and musicians, to leaders and visionaries, personalities born under the Aries sign have made significant contributions to the world. Their legacies continue to inspire us and shape our world.

As we delve into the stories of these Aries individuals we will explore their concise biographies and distinctive Aries traits that define their impact. Join us as we celebrate the spirit and accomplishments of these individuals born under the sign of Aries.

CHARLIE CHAPLIN

- Date of Birth; April 16 1889.
- Brief Biography; Charlie Chaplin was a legend in silent films who gained worldwide recognition for his comedic brilliance and unforgettable character. He achieved fame through his groundbreaking contributions to cinema by revolutionizing storytelling through films.
- Aries Traits; Assertive and creative.

- Impact; Chaplins legacy lives on as a trailblazer, in the realm of film comedy. He is a revered cultural icon.
- Personal Life; Chaplin led a life marked by multiple marriages and controversies. However he left an enduring imprint on the entertainment industry.

DIANA ROSS

- Date of Birth; March 26 1944.
- Brief Biography; Diana Ross is an singer, actress and record producer renowned for her powerhouse voice and contributions to Motown. Through her role as the vocalist of The Supremes and her successful solo career she has achieved many chart topping hits.
- Aries Traits; Energetic and determined.
- Impact; Diana Ross holds influence in the music industry as an embodiment of empowerment.
- Personal Life; Ross enjoys a fulfilling family life alongside a career that spans decades.

ROBERT DOWNEY JR.

- Date of Birth; April 4 1965.
- Brief Biography; Robert Downey Jr. Is an actor acclaimed for his versatility in roles and exceptional talent. He garnered worldwide acclaim for his portrayal of Tony Stark/Iron Man, in the Marvel Cinematic Universe.
- Aries Traits; Charismatic, adventurous and creative.
- Impact; Downeys performances have made a lasting impression on film leaving a significant mark.
- Personal Life; In his personal life he has overcome many challenges and is well known for his philanthropic endeavors.

LUCY LAWLESS

- Date of Birth; March 29 1968.

- Brief Biography; Lucy Lawless is an actress and singer from New Zealand. She is most famous for her portrayal of Xena in the television series "Xena; Warrior Princess."
- Aries Traits; Fearlessness, determination and charisma.
- Impact; Lawless has become a symbol of empowerment. She has paved the way for the inclusion of powerful women characters in the entertainment industry.
- Personal Life; In her personal life she continues to act while also advocating for social and environmental causes.

THOMAS JEFFERSON

- Date of Birth; April 13 1743.
- Brief Biography; Thomas Jefferson was one of America's Founding Fathers serving as the author of the Declaration of Independence and later becoming the nation's President.
- Aries Traits; Intellectuality, visionary thinking and determination.
- Impact; Jefferson's legacy includes expanding the nation through the Louisiana Purchase while strongly championing liberties.
- Personal Life; Thomas Jefferson had personal interests in architecture, science and farming.

MARIAH CAREY

- Date of Birth; March 27 1969.

- Brief Biography; Mariah Carey is a singer, songwriter and actress who is widely recognized for her extraordinary vocal range. Throughout her career she has produced chart topping hits and solidified herself as one of the most influential female artists in the music industry.
- Aries Traits; Known for being creative, ambitious and independent.
- Impact; Mariah Carey's musical contributions have left an indelible mark on the industry. Her vocal prowess is highly acclaimed by critics and fans. Additionally she has won numerous Grammy Awards.
- Personal Life; She has found fulfillment in her personal life with a loving family.

ERIC CLAPTON

- Date of Birth; March 30 1945.
- Brief Biography; Eric Clapton is a guitarist, singer and songwriter celebrated for his exceptional skills on the guitar. With a legendary status in rock music history he has played with influential bands like The Yardbirds and Cream before establishing himself as a successful solo artist.
- Aries Traits; Recognized as determined, passionate and innovative.
- Impact; Eric Clapton's mastery of the guitar has permeated generations of musicians. He is widely regarded as one of the greatest guitarists of all time due to his influence on the genre.
- Personal Life; Eric Clapton has led a life, marked by his musical achievements, as a highly regarded

guitarist and songwriter. However he has also faced challenges such as addiction and turbulent relationships. In addition he has been active in philanthropy.

LADY GAGA

- Date of Birth; March 28 1986.
- Brief Biography; Lady Gaga, whose real name is Stefani Joanne Angelina is a singer, actress and songwriter known for her unique style and popular music. Throughout her career she has received numerous awards and recognition for her contributions to pop culture.
- Aries Traits; Known for her bold and pioneering spirit, as well as her confidence, creativity, and determination.
- Impact; Lady Gaga is also an advocate for self expression and inclusivity.
- Personal Life; Lady Gaga's personal life is defined by her career as a singer, actress and activist.

ELTON JOHN

- Date of Birth; March 25 1947.
- Brief Biography; Elton John is a singer songwriter, pianist and composer renowned for his music and flamboyant stage presence. His illustrious career spans decades of timeless hits and multiple accolades that have solidified his status as a music legend. In addition to his achievements
- Aries Traits; Elton John possesses Aries qualities such as ambition, creativity and a captivating stage

presence. These attributes have greatly influenced his music career and philanthropic endeavors.
- Impact; Elton John has made contributions to the LGBTQ+ community through both his artistry and philanthropic endeavors.
- Personal Life; Elton John's had struggles with addiction and mental health. He is notable for his philanthropy.

J. P. MORGAN

- Date of Birth; Born on April 17 1837.
- Brief Biography; J. P. Morgan was a financier, banker and philanthropist who played an important role in shaping the financial system of the United States.
- Aries Traits; determined and strategic.
- Impact; Morgans influence in finance and industry had a major effect on the growth of the United States.
- Personal Life; He was widely recognized both in the world and American society as a pioneer of finance.

MARIA SHARAPOVA

- Date of Birth; Born on April 19 1987.
- Brief Biography; Maria Sharapova is a retired tennis player who achieved prominence as one of the top athletes in her sport. She secured Grand Slam titles and gained a reputation for her fierce competitive spirit.
- Aries Traits; Competitive, determined and confident.

- Impact; Sharapova's success and international recognition significantly contributed to the rise in popularity of women's tennis.
- Personal Life; Following her tennis career she ventured into business pursuits.

ARETHA FRANKLIN

- Date of Birth; Born on March 25 1942.
- Brief Biography; A Musical Legend, Aretha Franklin was a singer, songwriter and pianist who earned the title of "Queen of Soul." Throughout her career she captivated audiences with her iconic voice and unforgettable songs.
- Aries Traits; Aretha Franklin, showcased Aries qualities of determination, confidence and a strong pioneering spirit.
- Impact; Her talent and passion led to awards and accolades solidifying her status as a legend in the

music industry. She also actively participated in causes making contributions to the civil rights movement.

- Personal Life; Aretha Franklin actively participated in the civil rights movement. Unfortunately she faced health challenges, including diabetes before her passing in 2018.

In summary, this chapter explored how individuals born under this zodiac sign have left a legacy in the world. Their determination, creativity and unwavering passion have propelled them to greatness in fields. As we conclude our exploration of these Aries figures across entertainment, politics, sports and more; it is evident that they have not influenced our culture but also inspired generations with their unique journeys. Their unwavering determination and fearless approach to challenges have not only propelled them towards success. It has also created a lasting impact that continues to influence and inspire many more people.

As we acknowledge the achievements of these individuals born under the Aries zodiac sign, let their stories remind us of the qualities associated with this sign. Bravery, leadership and an unwavering pursuit of their dreams. These traits possess the potential to lead to accomplishments and contribute to change in our world.

Whether you share the Aries sign or simply appreciate the resilience and creativity of these individuals, their journeys ignite within you a pursuit of your own aspirations leaving an indelible mark on the fabric of life. As we bid farewell to this chapter let us carry the spirit of Aries with us as we face our own challenges, with determination and boundless enthusiasm.

CONCLUSION

We have reached the conclusion of our journey across Aries. Let us now take a moment to revisit the points we've discussed throughout this book. We want to appreciate the qualities of Aries individuals and offer them encouragement to embrace their traits. Before that let's summarize what we've learned about Aries.

Aries being the sign of the zodiac is known for its courage, assertiveness and unwavering pursuit of goals. Throughout this book we have uncovered the origins, history and mythology of Aries in various cultures. We have explored how they approach love, friendships and family dynamics. We have also delved into their career aspirations and personal growth while catching a glimpse into what lies ahead for them in the year. Additionally we have celebrated personalities who were born under the sign of Aries and left an impact on the world.

As we bring this book to a close it's time to wrap up everything we've covered and provide a sense of completion. We have journeyed through chapters each offering a perspective on the multifaceted nature of individuals born under Aries;

- **In Chapter 1** we traced back Aries through history and mythology unearthing ancient tales and beliefs associated with this sign.

- **In Chapter 2** we explored how Aries approaches love by providing insights into their compatibility and relationships.
- **In Chapter 3** we explored the dynamics of Aries when it comes to friendships and family, thereby providing guidance on how to nurture these connections.
- **In Chapter 4** we delved into Aries career preferences, strengths and challenges offering insights into their goals.
- **In Chapter 5** our focus shifted to Aries journey of self improvement. We provided exercises and guidance for personal growth and development.
- **In Chapter 6** we provided a glimpse into what the upcoming year ahead holds for Aries. We discussed key events and their potential impact.
- **In Chapter 7** we celebrated personalities who shared the Aries sign and explored their lasting legacies.

Our aim throughout these pages has been to honor the qualities of Aries individuals, inspire self awareness and offer insights into their multifaceted nature. We promised a guide to all aspects of Aries. From their origins to their love life family dynamics, career aspirations, personal growth journeys and encounters with astrological influences. If there's one thing we want you as a reader to take away from this book is this; Embrace your Aries spirit, with confidence and authenticity. Recognize that your assertiveness, passion and fearlessness are assets as you navigate through life.

The Aries zodiac sign, with its complexities, plays an important role in the vast tapestry of the universe. By understanding your qualities and embracing the spirit of Aries you can effectively navigate life's obstacles and achieve success in your endeavors. In conclusion it is important to keep in mind that astrology serves as a tool for self discovery and personal development. Ultimately the actions and decisions you take will shape your life.

We sincerely appreciate your participation in this journey alongside us. As you move forward may the knowledge gained from these pages continue to provide guidance while the celestial stars above illuminate your path towards an fulfilling life. May your cosmic expedition be filled with moments of discovery, personal growth and an enhanced connection to the universe surrounding us. Best wishes to you, Aries!

Subscribe To Sofia Visconti

As a subscriber you will receive a <u>Free Gift</u> + You wil be the first to hear about new books, articles and more exclusives **just for you**

Click Here

Or Visit Below:
https://www.subscribepage.com/svmyth

Or Simply Scan The Qr Code To Join

Printed in Great Britain
by Amazon